"*The Shapes are Real* is not merely a book of poetry, nor, even less, a sculpture catalog rendered in verse. Rather, it is a composite experience in which two creative presences—the sculptor and the poet—deliberately renounce the self-sufficiency of their respective languages and choose instead to inhabit a liminal space: one where form becomes spirit, and the word—a subtle material. Liviu Mocan does not offer recognizable objects, but ontological markers. His sculptures do not illustrate a vision—they contain it. They are signs, spiritual gestures embodied in metal, in wood, in stone, but most of all, in absence—because at the heart of each volume lies a dense silence, an unspoken question. Within this space open to the vertical, Jill Peláez Baumgaertner arrives not to explain, nor to extol, but to listen and respond—with a poetry that refuses spectacle yet seeks at every turn a quiet revelation. This book thus becomes not a juxtaposition of art forms, but a convergence of intuitions. Not a tandem, but a deep accord. Here, sculpture is no pretext, and poetry no reflection; they coexist as two hemispheres of the same act of faith—that beyond the visible, beyond the contingent, there exists a beauty that redeems, a shape that cannot be undone. A book about ascension—not through escape, but through a deepening into the real form of things."

—**Pavel Șușară**, Art Critic

"The exquisite arrangement of sculpture and poetry in this book offers such a profound experience of both pleasure and spiritual depth that I am left almost at a loss for words. In the time you spend with the book, you will find an alternative to the trivial and the terrible that sometimes seem to dominate current American life. Like me, maybe you, too, will pick this book up over and over to re-experience its breathtaking vision. Get two copies: one to keep and one to give to someone you love."

—JEANNE MURRAY WALKER, Poet

"After living through communism and the Cold War, a time of suppression and restraint for artists, Livu Mocan emerged stronger and more creative than ever. Now this pairing with the poet Jill Baumgaertner gives a buoyant example of the power of art set free. Poets compress meaning into words on a flattened page. Sculptors search for new media—wood, brass, marble, bronze, gold, iron, sandstone, walnut, oak—to express the same truth in multiple shapes. Together, they offer a feast for the eyes and the mind."

—PHILIP YANCEY, author of *Where the Light Fell: A Memoir*

"Philosophers have written entire libraries about the unity between image and word. In the verses of the American poet and in the sculptures of the Romanian artist, we have a happy creative affinity, springing from a spiritual affinity and from the same Christian ideals. The whole world tends in the soul of the two authors towards the heights, towards the throne of the Creator. Elevated forms, ascensional momentum, religiosity, which sustain spiritual burning, praise of those who long for the peace beyond nature, the peace that the Lord gives."

—ADRIAN POPESCU, Poet

"Adam, the firstborn, not from the womb but from clay, animated with divine breath, is given the amazing task of naming creation. How did words come to be placed, in the beginning, next to each reality, each creature, each feeling . . . ? I cannot help but think that it was a coincidence. Perhaps the poetic side that humanity has never lost was revealed to Adam then. And then, a thought comes to me, that some of Adam's descendants are divided into two: those who create images and forms and those who feel the need to decipher them through words, sometimes giving birth to poetry."

—**Virgil Scripcariu**, Sculptor

"Words 'can go only so far.' Baumgaertner's ekphrastic poetry and Liviu Mocan's remarkable sculpture reach toward 'the ladder's top,' 'suggest what lies beyond / what lies ahead.' Beautifully produced, the book's poems and sculpture enhance appreciation of their shared vertical, heavenward thrust. Each adroitly interweaves images of creation, planting, and crucifixion. Each is 'always about ascending.' What 'we cannot do . . . / ourselves' this marriage of sculpture and poetry facilitates in a book for pondering, prayer, and praise."

—**Bonnie Thurston**, author of *Saint Mary of Egypt: A Modern Verse Life and Interpretation*

"Jill Peláez Baumgaertner's poems in *The Shapes Are Real* are moving meditations inspired by the work of Romanian sculptor Liviu Mocan. Like the shapes this book celebrates, Baumgaertner's poems present themselves almost as three-dimensional objects, intricately-made linguistic engines that generate energy implicit in the art the poet beholds. Images of ladders, pillars, and crosses abound, moving the earthbound reader's gaze upward towards the infinite and the (im)possible: 'We stand in earth, in dust, / and reach for shapes / we see through mist.' The vertical thrust of Baumgaertner's powerful lyrics reminds us that words, like the Word himself, serve as both means of conveyance and destination, and constitute a kind of parousia. The fortunate reader realizes, to paraphrase the words of Emily Dickinson, surely one of the tutelary spirits of this volume, 'instead of getting to heaven, at last—/ we're going, all along.'"

—**Angela Alaimo O'Donnell**, author of *Holy Land*

THE SHAPES ARE REAL

The Poiema Poetry Series

Poems are windows into worlds; windows into beauty, goodness, and truth; windows into understandings that won't twist themselves into tidy dogmatic statements; windows into experiences. We can do more than merely peer into such windows; with a little effort we can fling open the casements, and leap over the sills into the heart of these worlds. We are also led into familiar places of hurt, confusion, and disappointment, but we arrive in the poet's company. Poetry is a partnership between poet and reader, seeking together to gain something of value—to get at something important.

Ephesians 2:10 says, "We are God's workmanship..." *poiema* in Greek—the thing that has been made, the masterpiece, the poem. The Poiema Poetry Series presents the work of gifted poets who take Christian faith seriously, and demonstrate in whose image we have been made through their creativity and craftsmanship.

These poets are recent participants in the ancient tradition of David, Asaph, Isaiah, and John the Revelator. The thread can be followed through the centuries—through the diverse poetic visions of Dante, Bernard of Clairvaux, Donne, Herbert, Milton, Hopkins, Eliot, R. S. Thomas, and Denise Levertov—down to the poet whose work is in your hand. With the selection of this volume you are entering this enduring tradition, and as a reader contributing to it.

—D.S. Martin
Series Editor

THE SHAPES ARE REAL

Poems on Sculptures of Liviu Mocan

JILL PELÁEZ BAUMGAERTNER

*Forewords by Philip Yancey
and D. S. Martin*

CASCADE Books · Eugene, Oregon

THE SHAPES ARE REAL
Poems on Sculptures of Liviu Mocan

Poiema Poetry Series

Copyright © 2025 Jill Peláez Baumgaertner. All rights reserved. Except for brief quotations in critical publications or reviews, no part of this book may be reproduced in any manner without prior written permission from the publisher. Write: Permissions, Wipf and Stock Publishers, 199 W. 8th Ave., Suite 3, Eugene, OR 97401.

Cascade Books
An Imprint of Wipf and Stock Publishers
199 W. 8th Ave., Suite 3
Eugene, OR 97401

www.wipfandstock.com

PAPERBACK ISBN: 979-8-3852-4584-0
HARDCOVER ISBN: 979-8-3852-4585-7
EBOOK ISBN: 979-8-3852-4586-4

Cataloguing-in-Publication data:

Names: Baumgaertner, Jill Peláez.
Title: The shapes are real : poems on sculptures of Liviu Mocan / Jill Peláez Baumgaertner.
Description: Eugene, OR: Cascade Books, 2025 | Series: Poiema Poetry Series | Includes bibliographical references.
Identifiers: ISBN 979-8-3852-4584-0 (paperback) | ISBN 979-8-3852-4585-7 (hardcover) | ISBN 979-8-3852-4586-4 (ebook)
Subjects: LCSH: Poetry. | Christian poetry.
Classification: PN1010 B38 2025 (paperback) | PN1010 (ebook)

VERSION NUMBER 08/15/25

For Michael Wilder,
the gifted musician, whose artistic vision
brought poet and sculptor together

When we make, we invoke the abundance of God's world into the reality of scarcity all about us.

—Makoto Fujimura

Contents

Illustrations ix
Foreword Polishing Mirrors for Heaven by Philip Yancey xiii
Foreword by D.S. Martin xvii

Prologue
The Birth of Poetry 3

Ladders
Ascension I 7
In Galleries: The Ladder of All Jacobs 10
Beyond Pain: *King's Ladder* 12
Ecce Homo! (1) 14
Golgotha 17
After the Annunciation: *The Second Adam* 21
Heaven's Eyes 23
Kathy's Dream/*Jacob's Ladder* 26
Tree of Love/Tree of Life 28

Pillars
The Sin 33
Trinity 35
Shot Pillars 37
Vertical Libraries 38
Decalogue 40

Seeds
The flowers die too, don't they? 45
The Birth of Stained Glass 48
Sunday Morning I 50
Sunday Morning II 52

Sunday Morning III 54
Sunday Morning IV 56
Ascension II 58
Sowing Poems: *Seed Among Thorns* 60
Illseed 62
Deliverance 64
Little Seed: Eva becomes Ave 66

Five Solas
The book that reads you 69
Anchor cast up to heaven 71
The Lamb of God 73
The ladder of the world 75
The Trumpet in the Universe 78
A Tombstone, the sixth archetype 81

Epilogue
Altar for the book of words, Altar for the book of nature 85

Notes 87
Acknowledgments 89

Illustrations

The Birth of Poetry 2
bronze, h. 121 cm.
Dedicated to Jill Baumgaertner

Ascension I 6
cherry, pine, beech, lead, 199x19x20 cm.

The Ladders of All Jacobs 9
walnut, sandstone, h. 40 cm.

King's Ladder 11
iron, h. 300 cm.

Ecce Homo! (A letter to Leonardo) 13
iron, zinc, h. 279 cm.

Golgotha 16
oak, iron, granite of Poieni, water, h.900 cm
Collection of Cojocna commune town hall, Cluj county, România

The Second Adam 20
iron, zinc, h. 277 cm.

Heaven's Eyes 22
iron, h. 300 cm. Collection of the Art Museum of Timișoara, România

Jacob's Ladder 25
bronze, stone, wood, h. 40 cm.

Tree of Life 27
iron, zinc, h.300 cm.
Collection of Aletheea Center, Timișoara, România

The Sin 32
oak, gold, iron, h. 245 cm.
Collection of Cristian and Liliana Moisescu, România

Trinity 34
iron, zinc,. h. 293 cm.
Collection of Nigel and Sue Holliday, U.K.

Vertical Libraries 39
(Mathew, Mark, Luke and John)
gold, bronze, iron, paper, h. 253 cm.
The bronze one, collection of Babeș-Boliay University, Cluj-Napoca, Romania

Shot Pillars 36
(Romanian Anticomunist Revolution, 1989)
bronze, granite, h. 350 cm.
Collection of Cluj-Napoca Town Hall, România

Decalogue 42
gold on fiberglass, granite, grass, h. 460 cm.
Collection of Sun Garden Resort, Cluj-Napoca, România

The Flowers Die Too, Don't They? 44
bronze, granite, h. 155 cm.
Collection of Bogdan and Emma Stănescu, România

The Birth of Stained Glass 47
paper, cloth, stained glass, mirror, h. 234 cm.

Sunday Morning I 49
brass, oak, 190 x 20 x 20 cm

Sunday Morning II 51
plum, rusted iron, 23 x 30 x 130 cm
Collection of Mihai Frişan, România

Sunday Morning (III) 53
walnut, brass, gold, h. 134 cm.
Collection of Lucian and Alexandra Pop, România

Sunday Morning (IV) (detail) 55
cherry, gold, h. 221 cm.
Collection of Johan David and Ioana Raluca Bies, România

Ascension (II) 57
bronze, red Moneasa marble, h. 157 cm.
Collection of Graham W. Giles, U.K.

Seed Among Thorns 59
bronze, acacia, h. 150 cm.

Illseed 61
macrocarpa, h. 700 cm.
Collection of North Shore Hospital, Auckland, N.Z.

Deliverance (detail) 63
aluminum, tree, h. 199 cm.

Little Seed 65
bronze, h. 19 cm.
The trophy that the European Leadership Forum offers to its collaborators.

The Book that Reads You 68
(dedicated to Johannes Gutenberg)
brass, h. 120 cm.
Collection of Wheaton College, Wheaton, IL. USA

Anchor Cast up to Heaven 70
bronze, brass, iron, h. 460 cm.
Collection of L'abri England, Greatham, UK.

The Lamb of God 72
brass, h. 245 cm.

The Ladder of the World 74
brass, 3 x 2.39 x 1.26m
Collection of the Art Museum, Cluj-Napoca, România

Trumpet in the Universe 77
Brass, h. 540 x 120 x 120 cm.
Collection of Wheaton College, Wheaton, IL. USA

Tombstone 80, 81
sandstone, at Great St. Mary Church, Cambridge, UK, incorporated in "Archetypes" exposure.

Altar for the Book of Words, Altar for the Book of Nature 84
oak, h.267 cm.
Collection of Daniel Mezo and Cristina Marian, România

Foreword
Polishing Mirrors for Heaven

I have visited Russia twice. The first time, in 1991, I found a nation in deep chaos. The Soviet Union was rapidly disintegrating, and that year's news featured a failed coup against President Mikhail Gorbachev and the resulting power struggle led by Boris Yeltsin. Ultimately, Yeltsin would triumph over Russia's diehard communists, after leading a military attack on the parliament building and introducing a new era of freedom and openness to the West.

On my second visit, in 2002, I traveled to Saint Petersburg in order to attend a Christian book fair, itself an emblem of the changes that had swept across the country. By then, some 7000 missionaries had flooded into Russia, whose citizens now confronted a bewildering array of denominations and cults, each of which offered an alternative to the thousand-year traditions of the Russian Orthodox Church.

One afternoon I toured the renowned Hermitage Museum, spending most of my time in the magnificent gallery devoted to works by Rembrandt. I watched as teachers escorted groups of Russian schoolchildren into the room. They bravely tried to hold the fidgeting kids' attention while describing the various paintings, especially those with religious themes: *David and Jonathan*, *The Holy Family with Angels*, *Descent from the Cross*, *The Sacrifice of Isaac* and, most prominently, *Return of the Prodigal Son*.

Observing the groups of children, it struck me that despite 75 years of militant atheism—during which 42,000 priests had been killed and 98 percent of churches shuttered—Christianity had never departed from Russia. Icons and paintings, such as those by Rembrandt, kept alive the stories that had long been suppressed, and now ordinary schoolteachers were free to explain their message to a new generation.

Little did I know that Russia's window of religious freedom would soon slam shut. Already a new President, Vladimir Putin, was drafting laws that would result in the expulsion of all missionaries as "foreign agents" and restore the power of Russian Orthodoxy. In return, the Orthodox patriarch would become one of the main cheerleaders supporting the brutal invasions of Ukraine.

In subsequent years I visited other countries in the former Soviet orbit: Ukraine, Belarus, Kazakhstan, Bulgaria, Hungary, Poland, Czech Republic, Serbia, the three tiny Baltic countries—and Romania. In each of them I found a small but vibrant Christian community still exulting in the freedom to worship. And in Romania I met a remarkable artist named Liviu Mocan.

Hailing from Transylvania, a region known mainly as the setting for Dracula and other vampires, Mocan has gained international acclaim as a sculptor who brazenly focuses on religious themes. While I was speaking at a pastors' conference, he stood by my side, extemporaneously fashioning sculptures to illustrate what I was saying. Mocan became a dear friend, a larger-than-life artist who specializes in larger-than-life sculptures.

Mocan shatters the stereotype of the reclusive, introverted artist. In a restaurant, his booming voice and infectious spirit often take over the room. I've seen him move from table to table shaking hands and introducing himself to total strangers. One evening he hosted a banquet for fifty people in his home and somehow talked me into joining a group of Romanian dancers in local costumes.

Yet in his studio and forge, Mocan is all business. Besides the ancient craft of metal-working, he has also incorporated modern techniques such as computer-aided design, 3D printing, and laser cutting. When Romania held a contest to commemorate the demonstrators who were shot during protests against the dictator Ceausescu in 1989, Mocan's submission, "The Shot Pillars," won. It stands in his home city as a memorial to those who helped topple an oppressive regime.

Mocan studied art at a state-sponsored school in the 1970s, when he had to embed his works' meaning in a kind of code. Public expression of Christian faith was a serious crime under Ceausescu's rule in Romania. Now free to express himself openly, Mocan is happy to elucidate the messages and symbolism in his artwork.

One professor described Mocan's work as "reverse dadaism," a kind of antidote to existential despair. In an era when modern art often centers on themes of meaninglessness, violence, and sexuality, Mocan celebrates freedom, joy, and the lasting contributions of the Christian faith. Among his many awards, he received a national prize for "The Heart of Resurrection." In 2009 Switzerland commissioned him to create a monumental sculpture in Geneva to commemorate the 500th anniversary of John Calvin's birth.

A few years later Mocan made a set of brass sculptures to celebrate the essence of the Protestant Reformation—an ironic homage, since some reformers had stripped churches of artistic images. The series, titled "Reformation—The Five Solas" includes these pieces:

- *sola scriptura:* by scripture alone
- *sola fide:* by faith alone
- *sola gratia:* by grace alone
- *solus Christus:* through Christ alone
- *soli Deo gloria:* for God's glory alone

His series of sculptures on *scriptura alone* brings new life to the normally boring representation of printed books, especially the Bible. And Mocan takes seriously that last motif: "for God's glory alone," as seen in "The Trumpet in the Universe," now displayed at Wheaton College. God is the true artist, he insists, and we simply try to reflect back some of the beauty that God has lavished on earth.

"I am striving to polish mirrors for heaven," Mocan says about his work. "When my hands touch the marble or the granite or the wood, when my hands deepen in soft clay, I touch God's hands. God's hands are there waiting for me…This is how, resculpting His sculptures, I understand, day by day, how inadequate I am. I am a sculptor, I am a sculpture."

Mocan's work harks back to a time when the church both inspired and patronized the arts. Great examples have endured despite the sometimes-hostile history taking place around them. He stands in the tradition of Caravaggio, da Vinci, and Michelangelo, as well as Handel, Bach, Dante, and Milton.

In modern Europe and North America, the church is seldom seen as a font of inspiration for the arts. But as I saw in the Hermitage Museum, art can express faith in a durable way even when words are forced to fall silent. Perhaps decades from now Russian schoolchildren will be studying artists like Liviu Mocan as they learn about a faith that decades of atheism—or institutional religion—could not suppress.

—Philip Yancey

Foreword by D.S. Martin

There is a second important part to what Philip Yancey intended to eventually share concerning the art of Romanian sculptor Liviu Mocan, but for personal reasons has been unable to complete it. "Polishing Mirrors for Heaven" by Philip Yancey was intended to be a foreword to the book of poems by American poet Jill Peláez Baumgaertner, created and presented in partnership with Mocan's sculptures, entitled *The Shapes are Real* (Poiema/Cascade, 2025).

Baumgaertner is Professor of English Emerita at Wheaton College, where she served as Dean of Humanities and Theological Studies from 2001–2017. The connection began when Dr. Michael Wilder, Dean of Communication and Arts at Wheaton, shared photos with her of some of Liviu's work and expressed the desire to feature one of Liviu's sculptures in the lobby outside the concert hall in the newly built Armerding Center for the Arts at Wheaton College.

Jill and her husband were so taken with Liviu Mocan's sculptures, particularly "Solo Dei Gloria"—which Jill says is magnificent and perfect for the location—that they became the required donors to make this installation possible. They also later purchased Mocan's "The Book That Reads You" to be eventually placed in the newly designed library.

Jill Baumgaertner told me,

> "I got to know Liviu and his wife Rodica when they came for the dedication. We had dinner and lively conversation and in the process realized that we had identical, or at least very similar, ideas about the gift of creation that God so generously gives to artists—and the responsibility to praise him through our work and tell his stories and lift percipients to new understandings of his glory. We hatched the idea of collaborating on a book of photos of his sculptures and poems that I would write—not necessarily about the sculptures—but inspired by them."

This was a project she felt was important for her to complete, even though she had no idea whether it was something a publisher would be willing or able to take on. When Jill shared her poems with me—since I had been the editor for one of her earlier collections, *What Cannot Be Fixed* (Poiema/Cascade, 2014)—I could see that her approach to ekphrastic poetry was consistently more about capturing the spirit of the artwork than about merely documenting it.

In the opening stanza of a poem responding to "The Art of Poetry," a sculpture Liviu Mocan dedicated to Jill Baumgaertner, Jill writes:

> Before the words surface,
> before the first breath, they are all
> curls and stabs, floating there,
> porous, delicate as glass yet lethal,
> leaking danger but up up breathing at last
> a limber word that lightly
> brushes the bronze, the gift
> of radical syllables uttered and answered
> before they coalesce.

My eye goes from the poem to the image, and back to the poem again. It is as if the sculptor is responding to the poet as much as the poet is responding to the sculptor. In reality, both are responding to the vison they share of how Christian artists of whatever discipline let their God-dominated imaginations speak.

The sculptures, clearly stand on their own, and the poems work independently of the images. Even so, when they are considered together greater possibilities emerge.

Jill says, "We want our book to tell the story that begins in radiance and beauty, progressed through sin to the fall, and leads to revelation and redemption through the vast and tender love of Christ." This is exactly what they have accomplished.

I hope this essay now fulfils Philip Yancey's intentions for it—to be more than merely an introduction to a significant Christian sculptor, and more than a preview of Mocan's partnership with Jill Peláez Baumgaertner in her new poetry book *The Shapes are Real* (Poiema/Cascade, 2025).

Perhaps we might yet be on the verge of reviving our influence on the culture around us—harkening "back to a time when the church both inspired and patronized the arts."

PROLOGUE

Bronze, H 1.1 m

The Birth of Poetry

Before the words surface,
before the first breath, they are all
curls and stabs, floating there,
porous, delicate as glass yet lethal,
leaking danger but up up breathing at last
a limber word that lightly
brushes the bronze, the gift
of radical syllables uttered and answered
before they coalesce.

The words knife and name, they wing,
they Adam all with light,
gesturing, circling, pointing suspended
to what is palpable,
to pulse beating rhythms
from a real presence.

And then the poem:
Whispering grasses.
The river's current muscling light.
The wafting cottonwood fluff.
Circling, circling, first one way
then the other, the words such a tumble,
the words almost, almost spoken,
not quite heard. Then the drift,
the crossouts, the tents of inserts,
and the surprise of words detouring.

Approaching 400 years past, we read Baxter:
"What will thy glory be!
My knowledge of that life is small."

But here, here the dazzle
of the Worded words
suspended between up
and down, never scraping earth,
always pointing
toward one who says,
"Astonish, amaze, stupefy me."

LADDERS

cherry, pine, beech, lead
119 x 19 x 20 cm

Ascension I

It is always about ascending,
these structures of stone and metal.
We think *up* is absolute
until we begin the descent to the Antipodes
and all is reversed.

Like Dante climbing Satan's
back, so far from God yet turning
over at the center of the earth,
beginning the descent,
grace bestowed in his turning.

And what I offer are words
which can go only so far,
often reaching the ladder's top
where they of course must stop
unable to say what cannot

be said but can only through
their silences and hesitations
suggest what lies beyond
what lies ahead.
Like words, time stalls.

We are caught. But sculptures
are now and reveal the maker.
Like the stones of Brodgar
that mark the earth with mystery,
their movers, gone, but they knew

the Ring's skyward reach,
and built them anchored
in the mud of earth but stretching
toward the light so real
they felt its glance upon their skin.

walnut, sandstone
h. 40 cm

In Galleries: The Ladder of All Jacobs

Ladders proliferate and tease
for a hand over hand and foot climb
to the top. The climb would be hopeful
if precarious, the promise the summit.
Which, however, never arrives in this lifetime.

The goal: to escape gravity, to mimic Jacob's
angels, Jesus as the ladder
and also the destination.
The ladder golden, Jacob sitting
on a bottom rung, the One above
at ladder's pinnacle, the One
to climb as he reveals the steps
and steadies a shifting balance.

Iron
300 x 50 x 50

Beyond Pain: *King's Ladder*

In his pain he sees the wrench
of it on her, his mother.
Her fists clench and re-clench.
Her mouth is a grim line,
stiff as a carved stick.
There is nothing she can do
and her mind is a white sheet
blank with ache. Only John
is there, no other children,
no other disciples. Only John
standing with the Marys.

Jesus, stretched open-armed
to the world, knows his mother's
agony, his friends' throb of grief
and helplessness. The blade
as sharp as death's scythe
carves into their hearts
and Jesus gives them to each
other, mother, son, linked
as witnesses, linked as sinners
standing as we stand under the cross.
Bereft together.

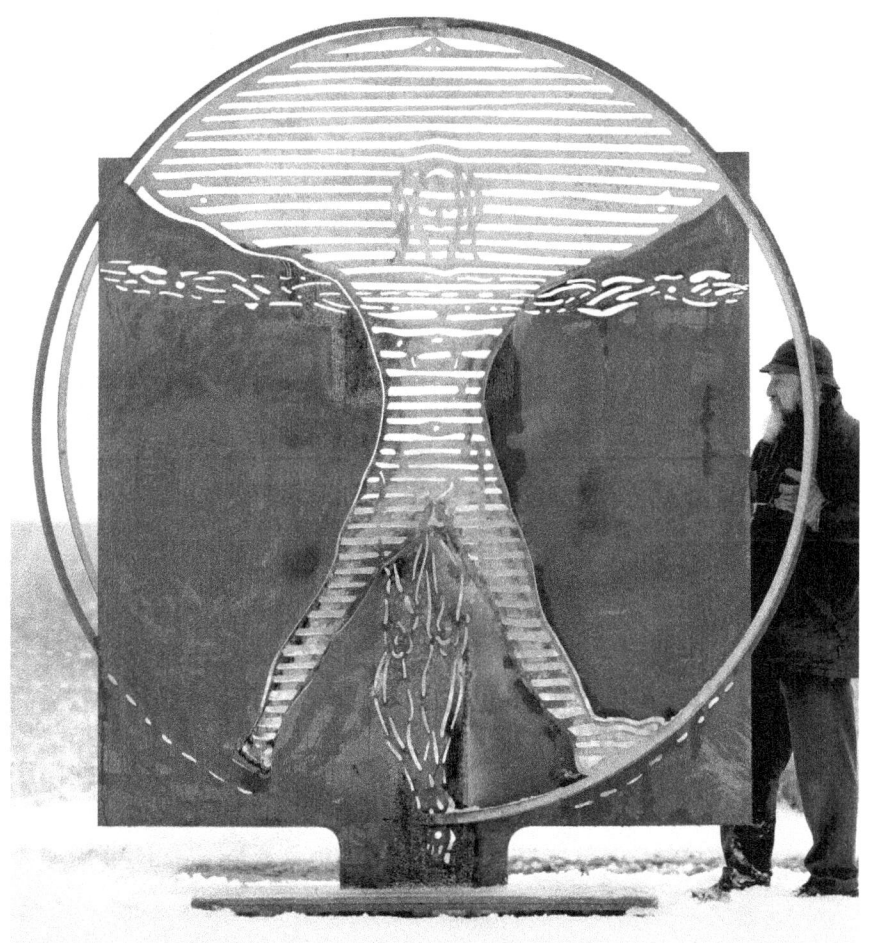

iron, zinc
148 x 136 x 35 cm

Ecce Homo! (1)

Always a man, this cross in a square
and ladder in a circle.
This man,
contained, confined, crossed.

It is somber, but it recalls
rolling in barrels down the hill,
roller coasters, tightropes,
jungle gyms, harlequins,
holy fools. And other fools,
Nietzsche for one, whose
final words before madness
were *Ecce Homo.*

And my father, too, no fool,
but no holy fool,
on the tennis court.
Sun on clay. No trees.
The oomph of balls on racquets.
The trophies lined up
in the bookcases.
The trophies that stymied us
after his death. What is to be done
with a father's trophies?
A memory of his steady cycle of strokes,
circles within squares.
He was caught in a ring of play,
of work, of balls back and forth.
of winning.

After his stroke, his balance shot,
his memory strong, he described
his P-38, the back and forth
from Italy to Germany, pictures
shot before bombing,
then again afterwards. 100 times.
No trophies here.
Just the Arlington 21 guns.

Ecce Homo. All humanity
and one man. Always one,
my father, yours, Christ
underlaid—a shadow to be
embraced or in many cases,
not.

But he hovers. He is a presence.
He cannot be played,
only climbed.

oak, iron, granite of poieni, water
h 900 cm

Golgotha

> *"Truly I tell you: today you will be with
> me in Paradise." Luke 23:43*

Jesus' hands are splayed
against the wood,
held fast, but each small
twitch of pain makes more pain.
Breathing is a task.
But still he breathes.
Enough to speak.

To the desperate cry of unbelief
from one of the crucified,
he closes his eyes.
But to the other who asks Jesus
to remember him,
he offers paradise. Today.

Paradise. So hard to grasp
amidst the clutter
of our days.
Could it be real? we ask,
so afraid it isn't.

But still we can imagine:
the scent of a garden of tomatoes,
the tiny prickles of soft rain,
the warmth of small breezes

on redeemed bodies.
The abundant fruit
and none forbidden.
And time for poems,
wrought in light
so shining we can finally see.
And time for music
in new tempos
and the euphonies
our earthly ears
could not take in.
And peaceful hours,
history finally dead.
And the clouds of witnesses,
not always seen but felt,
their multitudes
never crowding,
always standing,
sparking light,
sitting, even reclining
into the plush of grasses,
sometimes beside water
that seems still
yet moves like breath.

But one poet of the 20th century
is incredulous.
He finds abhorrent
a paradise where ripe fruit
never falls, where boughs
hang always heavy in the perfect sky.
"Death is the mother of beauty," he writes.
Nothing lasts. Nothing exists
beyond the grave. Nothing.
And that, he says,
creates the beauty
of the few hours we have.

But there is another way:
this dying Christ our only dying.
Our death behind us
in sprinkled water.

So much we do not know,
but this much is certain:
Christ forgave that thief
and drew him close.
Beauty blossomed
in the dark of Golgotha.
We stand in earth, in dust,
and reach for shapes
we see through mist.
The shapes are real.

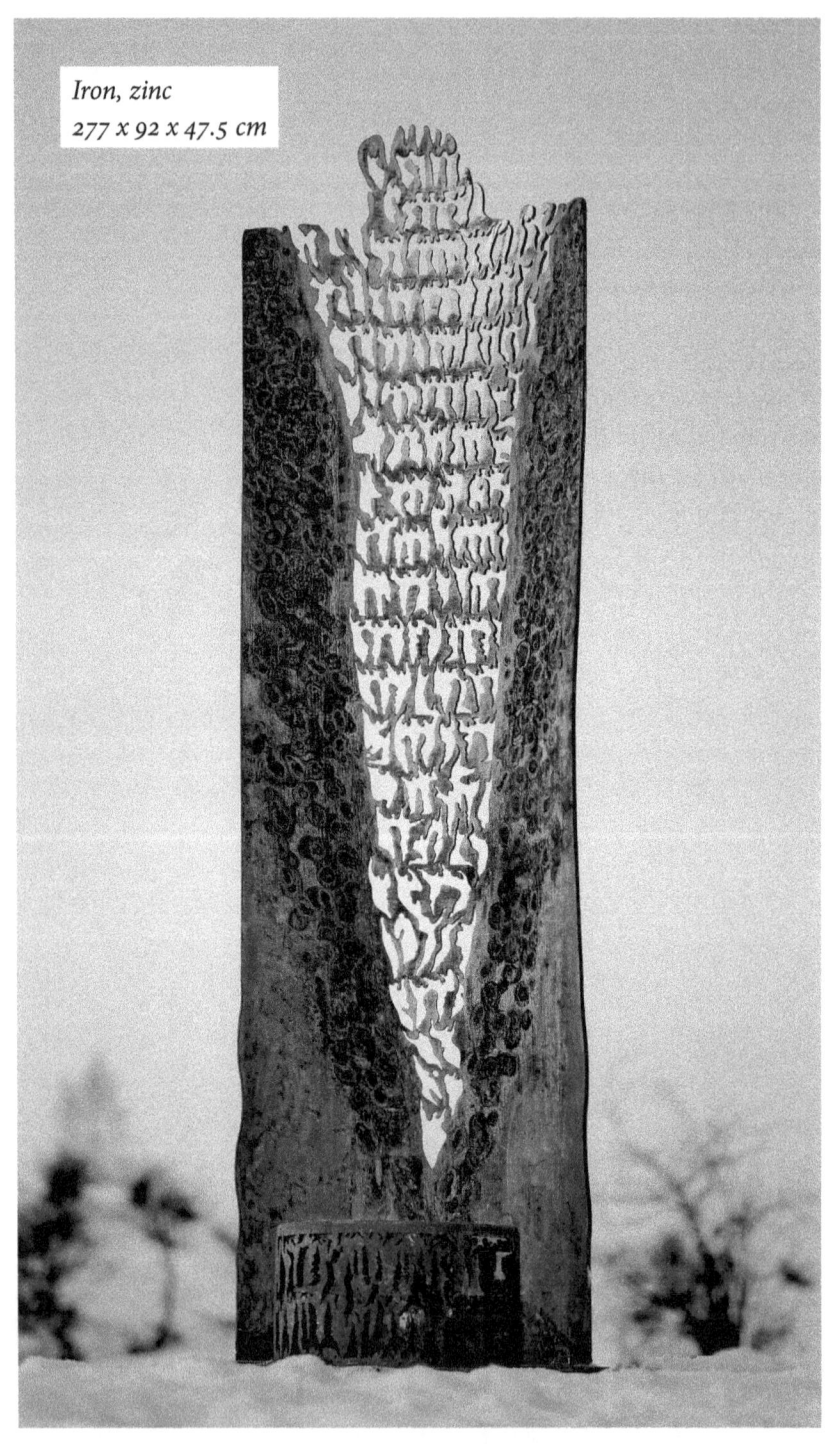

Iron, zinc
277 x 92 x 47.5 cm

After the Annunciation: *The Second Adam*

He tumbles, toeing the walls of his captivity,
hears her muffled chatter, tastes the fog
of the sweet foods she eats, is startled
by the noise of saw on wood, the pounding
of nails. The amniotic fluid in his throat
teaches him to swallow. Much later, he
learns pain as his neurons begin
to fire. This was before.

After, he upends us as he somersaults
our vision. Our words, yes, he as Word
words us. We taste the savor
of the bread, the spice of wine,
his lifeblood coursing our hearts' chambers.
He is pulse born. He is pulse borne.

His spirit muscles us, he lunges
for our breath. He is where we are.
He feels the lilts of our delights,
the blazes of our sufferings.

Fresh as new skin, taut as nerve strings,
he drums and whistles us, our beat, our melody.
Our bodies know his gifts,
Our everlasting bodies.

Iron 300 x 157 x 118 cm

Heaven's Eyes

These are not the eyes
of Doctor T. J. Eckleburg,
lifeless, looking out at the wasteland
like lotus seed pods.

This is the quickening gaze of one
who calls to life
the things that do not exist,
no slackening
        or break,
just mystery in the breath
and no breath, and flashes
of grace in and out of mist,
then suddenly a secret
        sunlit stretch of field.

At the end of his dock Gatsby
yearns for that faint light
across the bay. Redemption
        he thinks is recognition
and eros. It is wealth. The light
wavers in the haze.

But these other eyes steady,
a multitude of one,
a clutter of alert, of watching,
        of bringing to life all that lives,

of overwhelming presence solid
with vigilance, merciful
        even if we do not understand
the meaning

bronze, stone, wood
40 cm

Kathy's Dream/Jacob's Ladder

After a painting by Joel Sheesley

She stands facing away from us
        in a field of sky and grasses,
mesmerized by the geese ascending
and descending, which she accepts quietly.

Impossible, of course. They do not flutter
        up and down in the wide-awake world.
To take to flight or to land this field
they need space and a diagonal approach.

But in the dream they are a whirlwind
        of feathers, wings, intent.

Like angels opening the skies, showing the way,
        even Christ ascending and Kathy waiting
for his second descent, soft as doves,
silent, steady as that rock
        holding Jacob's weariness.

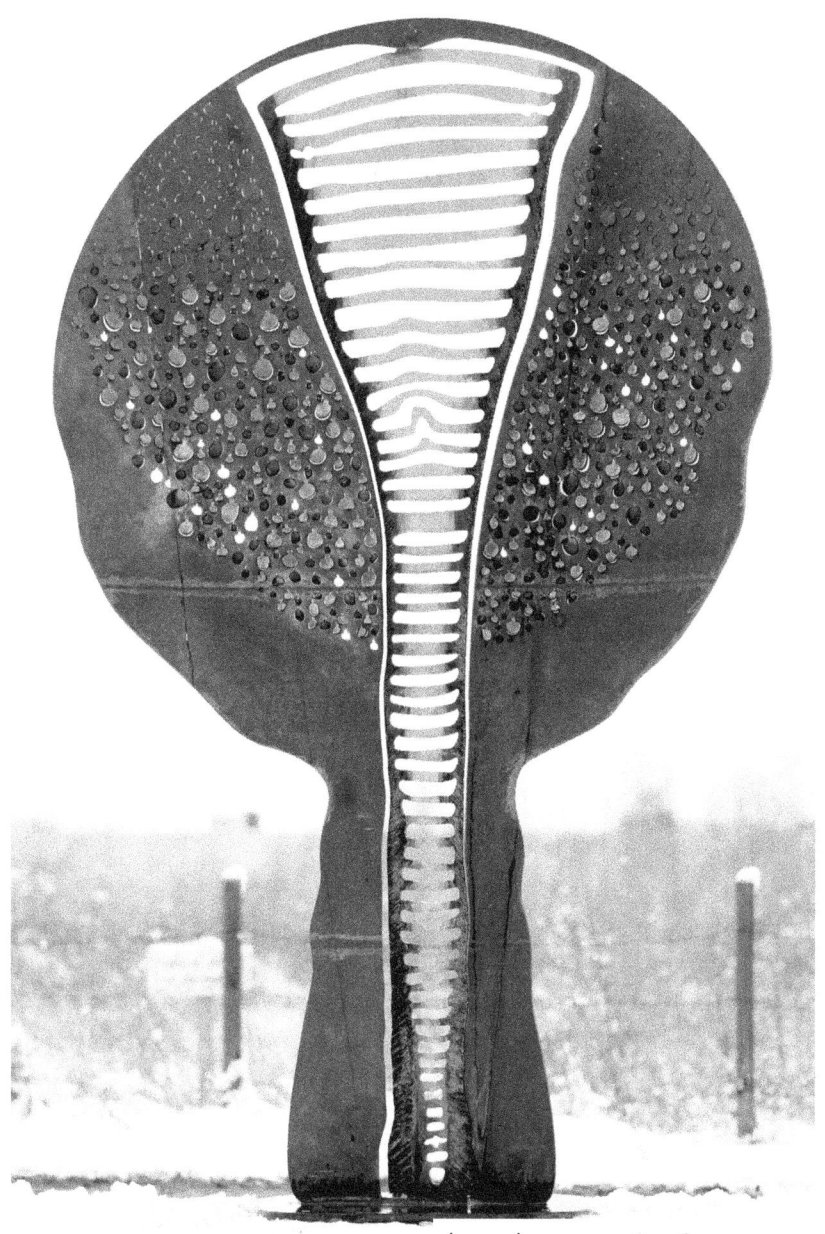

iron, zinc 300 x 167 x 85 cm

Tree of Love/Tree of Life

The iron tree trunked by a ladder
or is it a snake, all muscle
and stripes, the rungs the center,

the climb not for the living,
the snake a twist of intent.
Do we approach or hold back?

The apples so many tiny holes in iron,
in zinc, the gathering clouds glimpsed
through. Fruit early forming,

not to pick yet, others ready
for tasting. The tree of love,
the tree of life, a vast landscape.

The pastor's sermon on this day
was only barely about the country's
violence for which he said he had no

answers. Instead he described
the packages his mother would send—
occasional trinkets from the Dollar

Store, extra plastic forks, sometimes
the contents of a junk drawer,
each time an Ah! This!

And then his children's smiles
and their question, "Why?"
The tree of love has the answer.

The ladder stretches transforming
the wily creature to steps up, up.
The mother, ashes now,

but in the memory
is the randomness, the eccentricities.
She is climbing the tree of life,

the tree of love glinting
with the invitation
to touch, to taste and see

and always her rapt expression,
the clear brow,
the fragrant flesh of her.

PILLARS

oak, gold, iron
245 x 30 x 25 cm

The Sin

It coils around arms,
loops waist, neck.
It cannot be shaken
off, its hold tightening
to choking, to air bereft.

But now the cross skewers
the head, drives through
its small skull devoid
of imagination, just
impulses of deadly
strikes. It clings still,
its venom impotent
but pain a swagger
of knives behind its
eyes, crushed to death.

The cross a promise
beyond the pain
but still the pain
of breath.

iron, zinc
293 x 43 x 43 cm

Trinity

No fathoming.
No metaphors.
Each explanation falters.
Athanasius tried,
with many words.
Mere words will never do it
although poetry is sometimes
a ladder, the destination distant.

The artist takes on the impossible—
a sculpture of the Trinity. From this angle,
it seems, three arms hold
a globe, barely seen. The ladder
holds firm, a triangle, the most stable
structure, three sides,
no shifting, unbreakable.

No buckling. All one. All three.
And the earth held steady,
no torque at the joints.

Like music, absolute, beyond words,
beyond translation.

Like punctuation, silent,
except for the small breaths,
the tender stops, the jubilant
questionings.

Bronze

Shot Pillars

    (Romanian Revolution 1989)

Bare-chested they stood.
So easy, the pale flesh
sighted and triggered,
like bullets piercing
sponge, hearts exposed,
pulses mute.

And now the pillars
are as straight as bones.
They occupy the square
like standing stones, each
with a gouge large enough
for a hand.

Vertical Libraries

The sculptor's vertical
libraries are firm and steady.
Their pages fixed, they
never topple. But look!
They sometimes twist
at the pinnacle and their
meanings are skewed.

The books in my study
do not form pillars like these.
No neat stacks reaching
to the ceiling and no
regularly sized inventory.
Mine scatter across tables,
form random piles on desk,
sofa, floor.

      His books cannot
be read. How absolute they seem
as foundations, but the words
are invisible and as slippery
in their reach as the imagination.

Iron, sandstone, paper, gold

Decalogue

I was seven and my sister five
when we marveled at ten.
Our entry into ages that would keep us
enclosed for decades, although what

did we know about that?
Ten was magic, far away, impossible
with possibilities, filled
with mysteries and freedoms,

a blur of guesses. I counted
on my fingers, we counted
backwards from ten to signal starts
and finishes. Our fingers, still plump

with babyish grips and stretches,
were innocent of meaning,
including how those numbers worked,
not hexadecimal, octal, or binary

but decimal, digits, our fingers,
themselves a decalogue. Holy flesh
on tiny ones, not yet exposed to time
and its reckoning. Not yet aware of wrong

and the need for its constraints, hemmed in
by ten commands for work we did not know
and rest we did not need. Rest we simply
fell into each night. Mother, father

we embraced. We did no killing,
maybe the tiny lie when caught red-handed,
we did not scheme and plot to take away
each other's toys, the sabbath was holy

in its own way, and we did not know
other gods, just the one we prayed to
each night with mother by our side.
Our dolls were no idols, just frozen-faced

companions, dressed and undressed each day.
Now this decalogue invites us into its circle,
to sit amidst its geometry, its absolutes,
to stretch for freedoms outside its bounds

but never satisfactory. To crave gospel
made clear finally by limitations,
the utterly human, so prone to move in crooked
lines, though created good.

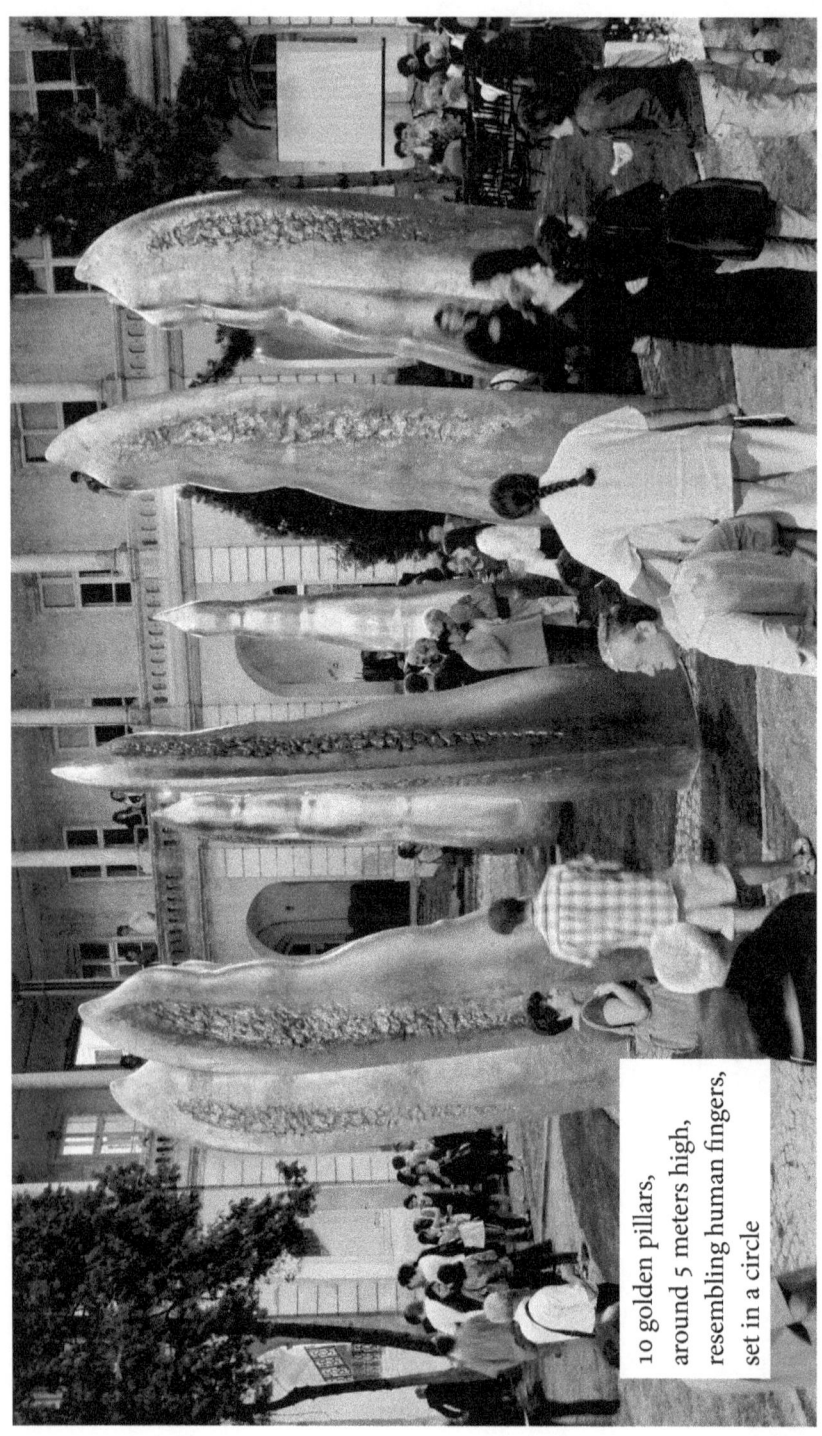

10 golden pillars, around 5 meters high, resembling human fingers, set in a circle

SEEDS

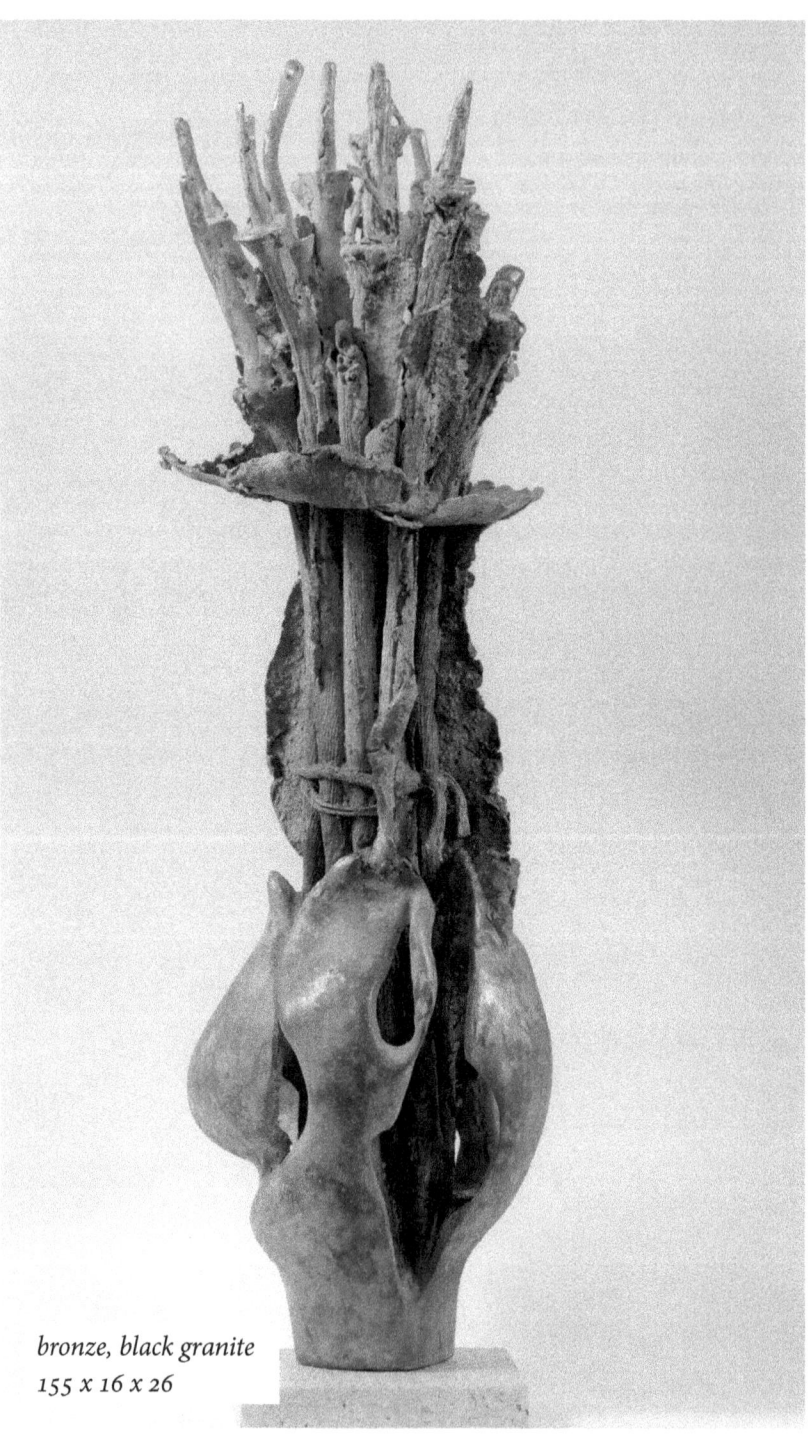

bronze, black granite
155 x 16 x 26

The flowers die too, don't they?

The oncologist had his say.
Then my mother:
"This can't be. This is a mistake.
A terrible mistake."

Her green dress,
her red lipstick,
her once slender fingers.

Toward the end
she was the writer,
dreaming her novel's
characters. She would
not let go their
perfections—
not admit their
flaws.

After the funeral
I found that tiny
tube of cream
that smoothed
her wrinkles. I
smeared it on my face,
coating myself
with her velvet,
her scent.

And opened her purse
to find her dusty
compact, her scratched
mirror, her tiny
brush with strands
of her hair,

and one ancient
handkerchief
embroidered
with flowers
not yet past
their bloom.

paper, cloth, stained glass mirror
234 x 21 x 21 cm

The Birth of Stained Glass

After Adam Zagajewski

All is left behind, finally we can agree,
but how can we leave Bach?
Who forges heaven's music
without him? Or perhaps that
is heaven's work. How will we hear it?
Will we fear it or thrill to its shivers?
Dissonances that tune differently,
maybe into dulce de leche.
Bells that become perfumes—
some sweet, some savory—and visions
that are heard as salt as all—all
of those birds singing raucously
in the arbor vitae on the terrace.

For now truth may be more in the oboes
and continuo, than in the priest's pronouncements,
or in our deep bows and genuflections—maybe
not in the light through glazed windows
casting rainbows of color on parishioners.
It is elsewhere. It is elsewhere.

brass, oak
190 x 20 x 20 cm

Sunday Morning I

The stamen of this Sunday morning's bloom
is a silent trumpet. The prelude has not begun.
We enter the vestry, reach for white
robes, cintures, knotted just so, our eyes
adapting to see by Paschal candle's light.

The morning is petals still unfolded. Psalms
still not chanted. The cross is waiting, waiting
to be lifted, the Book held high, the organ's
deepest tones stirring. The procession flowing,
a stream of living water to a tightened bud of promise.

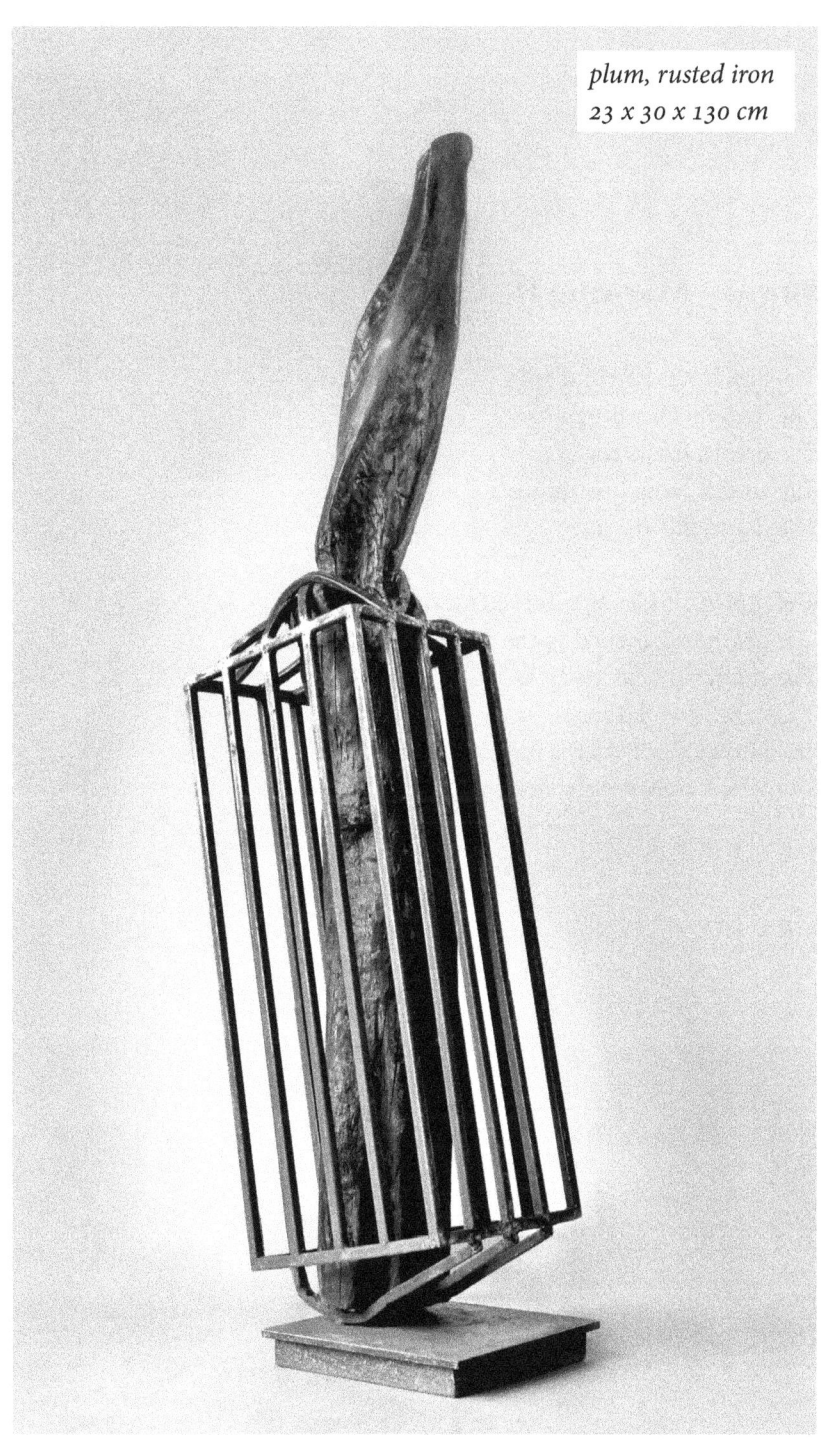

plum, rusted iron
23 x 30 x 130 cm

Sunday Morning II

The hungry droop and fall,
The dust fills the lungs,
The breath frosts the face,
The clouds hang brimming,
The damp fills the air.

The rain sprinkles the starved earth,
The death is drowned in the font.
The chalice is lifted to lips.
The haze is wiped from glass.
The knowledge inks the pages.
The Word breaks the shackles.

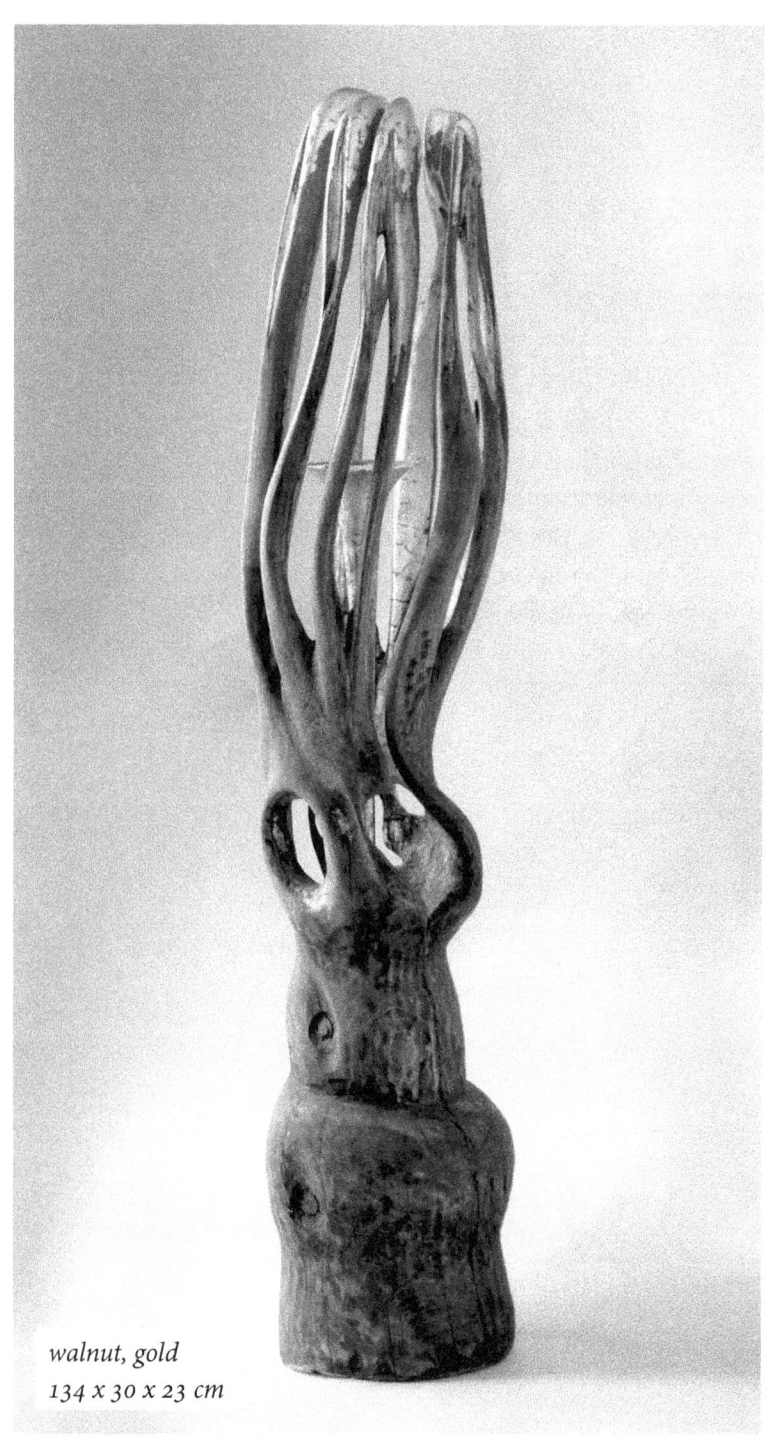

walnut, gold
134 x 30 x 23 cm

Sunday Morning III

This time breath wafts the fronds
and they bend slightly, like thin
Pentecost flames. The spikes of sin
have softened, the colors brighten,
the flower encloses the pollen-laden
bed found by a wandering bee
as he immerses his entire tiny body
in the richness; his minute hairs,
magnets for the pollen which he pushes
into his legs' pockets. Packed
for the journey.

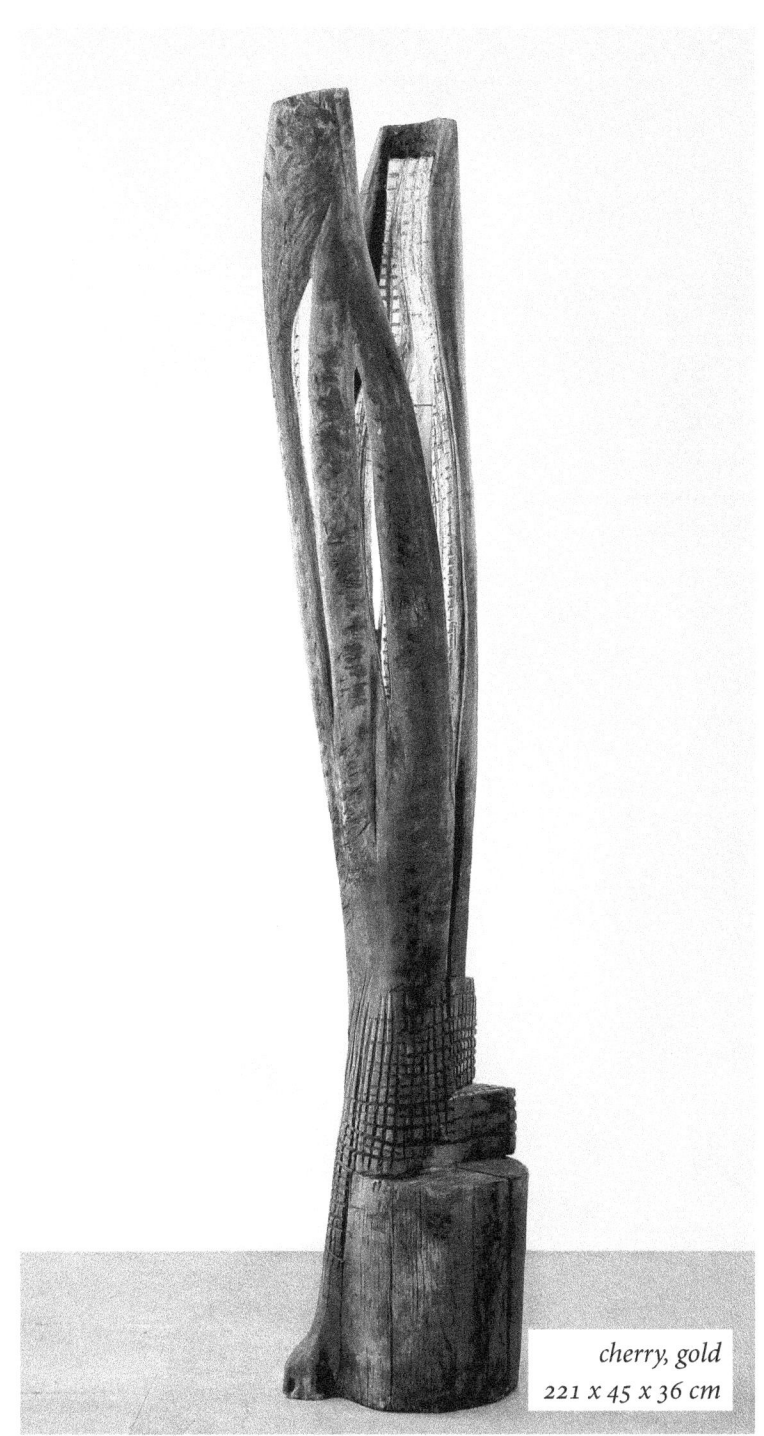

cherry, gold
221 x 45 x 36 cm

Sunday Morning IV

The garden in the deep night
after God's rapt silence
has no breath. No echo even
in the vacant tomb which no one
yet has visited, no one seen.
And yet everywhere his breathing,
the turn begins, the blanket
of sunrise in mist stretches
to swaddle the earth,
gouged and waiting.

bronze, red moneasa marble
157 x 16 x 16 cm

Ascension II

And all finally rises—dust, birds,
the gravity spurning the Up of growing things,
from hard seed, rough clod, to new
with the gleam of vertical.

The soil erupts up the green shoots,
to light, to fierce and mild,
to downing rain breaking through,
buds wrapped and straining for the bloom
to pillow the bee's search.

Each ascension from dormancy
means the cells have quenched their thirst,
the root birthed, the cells enlarging,
the cells dividing.

It is only after this rising,
Christ in the cloud,
this strong attraction to unfiltered light,
that the Spirit blossoms.

bronze, acacia
150 x 60 x 25 cm

Sowing Poems: *Seed Among Thorns*

the lines are fork tines,
thorns where a poem
balances
untethered
no roots no anchor

it could be wafted
like a thin plastic bag
floating a breeze
it will never erupt
through loam
it will never send forth
shoots   rhymes
stanzas filled
with more seeds
to scatter

it will defy fertility
it will never push
through green tubes
even pinprick blossoms
much less
glories of flora

it sits and waits
and all is silence
and night   no joy
no voices.

Macrocarpa, h 7m

Illseed

The poem's last lines must astound,
must not coast but shift into a breathless gear,
must rise from the lines' pyramid
as if planted in its center.

We do not expect this finish
and we do not hear the breathing,
no, the panting of those
whose pain is ephemeral;

we cannot hear because it was long ago.
But they brood around the pock-marked
obelisk, They are ill and still as seeds
waiting, waiting for their coat to break,

for the plumule to shoot
and the radicle to root,
the soil's surface to erupt,
the green lines to emerge

with nothing but promise, color, fruit.
The most true things we cannot understand.

aluminum, living tree
199 x 25 x20 cm

Deliverance

One thinks of the hard path
to birth, the seed in the column
encased in armor, and yet
after the difficult climb,
the sprouting, the blooming.

Encased in darkness—the bolts,
the strips of metal—the occasional
hint of light seeping through,
it does not seem promising,
but look up and see.

The breeze wafting the leaves,
the living tree connecting
earth and sky, bringing bones
to life, reassembling, giving access
to all the earth denies.

How will it be when atrophied
muscles pulse? When
collapsed lungs inflate
and veins and arteries begin
that living circulation?

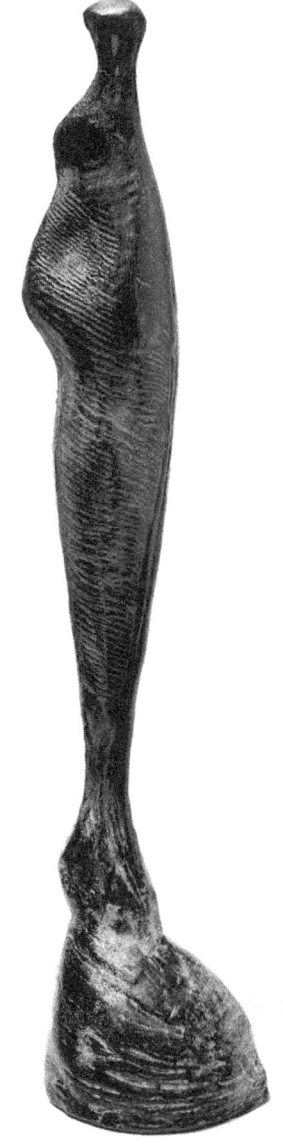

h. 19 cm

Little Seed: Eva becomes Ave

Jerome called her Eva,
Living One, life itself.
Without her without her sin
without her we would not live.
Without her Felix Culpa
as we fall, every heartbeat,
we would not have fallen.

She is a little seed,
a promise broken,
but still a promise hovering,
her hair tinged with gold
and with one hand
she holds the apple
she will bite,
spit seeds, swallow.

This little seed will rest
inside her until Mary
bends to spirit,
sprouts it. Ave.

FIVE SOLAS

brass
120 x 60 x 30 cm

The book that reads you

sees you; you standing there
trying to read its opaque pages;
stiff, unbendable they seem
yet stacked with abundance
of breath between leaves and brass
that seem almost flexible.

It eyes you. Over and over
through its hieroglyphs, the tiny eyes
see all that you are, all that you
should be, all that you will be.
They are not meaning—but point
to meaning, harbingers, reflectors,

like the light from the moon—
not sun but sunlight still—
reflected yet substantial,
until the morning erases
dark illuminations and unveils
glory—revelation the patina

covering sheen in the skin
of mercy.

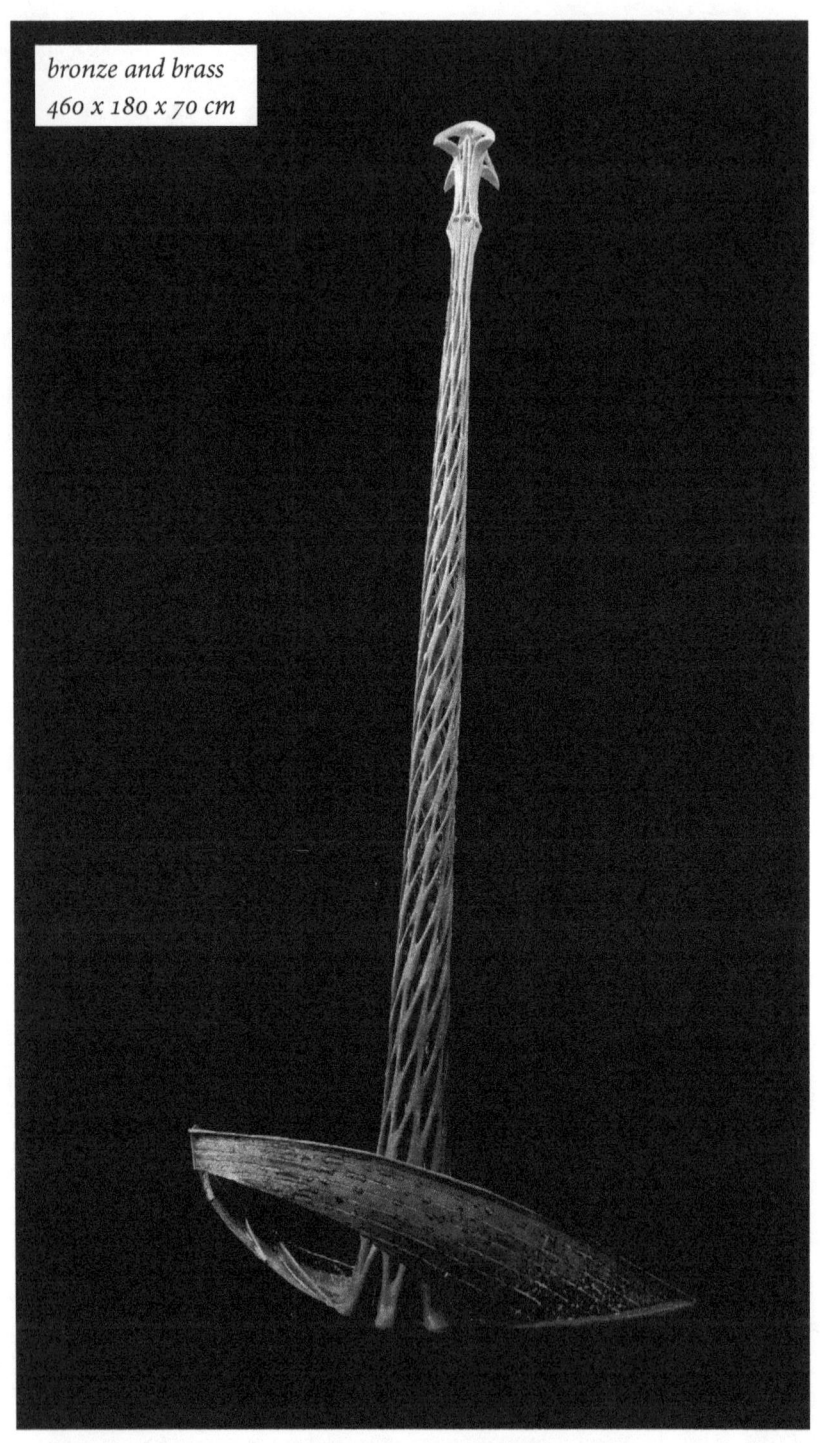

bronze and brass
460 x 180 x 70 cm

Anchor cast up to heaven

In this case, gravity is irrelevant.
Without this anchor, stretched to heaven,
the wrecked boat would sink,
chained to the depths of sin,
its fragile skin, broken,
the waters a gush of drowning.

But firm, straight, this rope—
the boat as delicate
and wind-tossed as paper,
or freshly dried hair.

Whoever cast this could shape it only
when it was hot-dipped galvanized,
drop-forged, hammered, red and smoking.

Who threw it higher than air,
and who is tugging it upward, upward,
the vessel, all of us,
at the end of the rope?

Only nails hammered could do this,
forged for one who cried, finally,
It is finished.

The finish our beginning. Our birth.

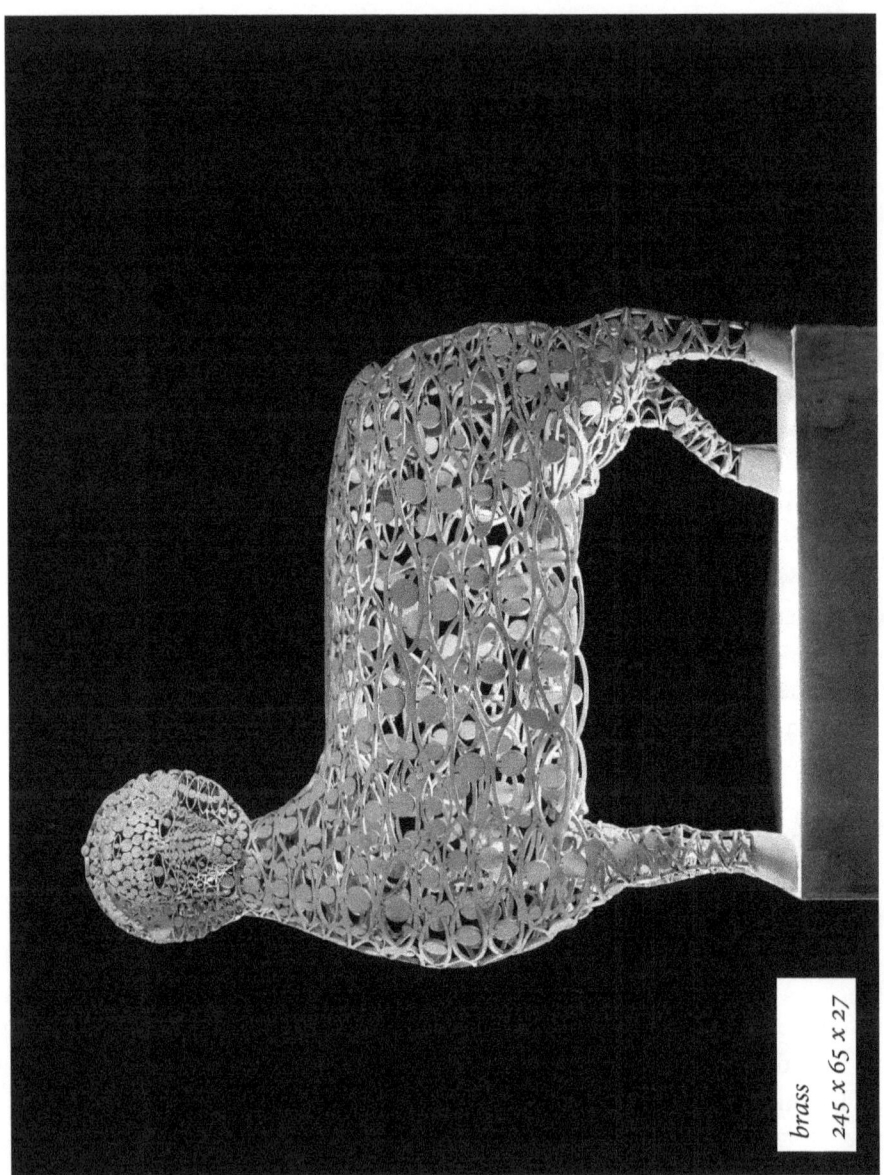

brass
245 x 65 x 27

The Lamb of God

is a curl of eyes and a dagger
in his breast, blanketed
with the pulse
of copper and zinc
cool to the touch.
The warmth of wool
is not for the present.
Upright, fraught with intention,
his head turned
to see all, each eye firm
to what comes next.

A lamb knows consumption
and hunger satisfied.
He is tender with love
and tough with pain. He looks
at us with his neck twisted,
his body erect and ready.

Seeing all in his calm gaze,
wise to our futile actions,
knowing we cannot do it
ourselves.

The lamb will do it.

brass
300 x 239 x 126 cm

The ladder of the world

has 49 layers of brass
and 365 rods. I climb
slowly, searching finger
grips and toe holds.

It is hard, this ascent,
but my grasp is not
the point. Christ
is steady. He does

not swerve. His toes
anchor earth. Ramrod
straight he is more
than a link.
He is vertical
and horizontal,
encompassing all—
arms stretched
to hold my cling.

This Christ does not
hold gently.
He is all angles
and corners, stiff,
unmoving. The ladder
is sharp
and painful.

But this rigid God
Is no idol. Nor is he
immovable.
With his bludgeoned
arms he reaches
the reluctant,
the recalcitrant,
the unmoved.
He reaches.
We stretch.

The climb is not
what gets us there.

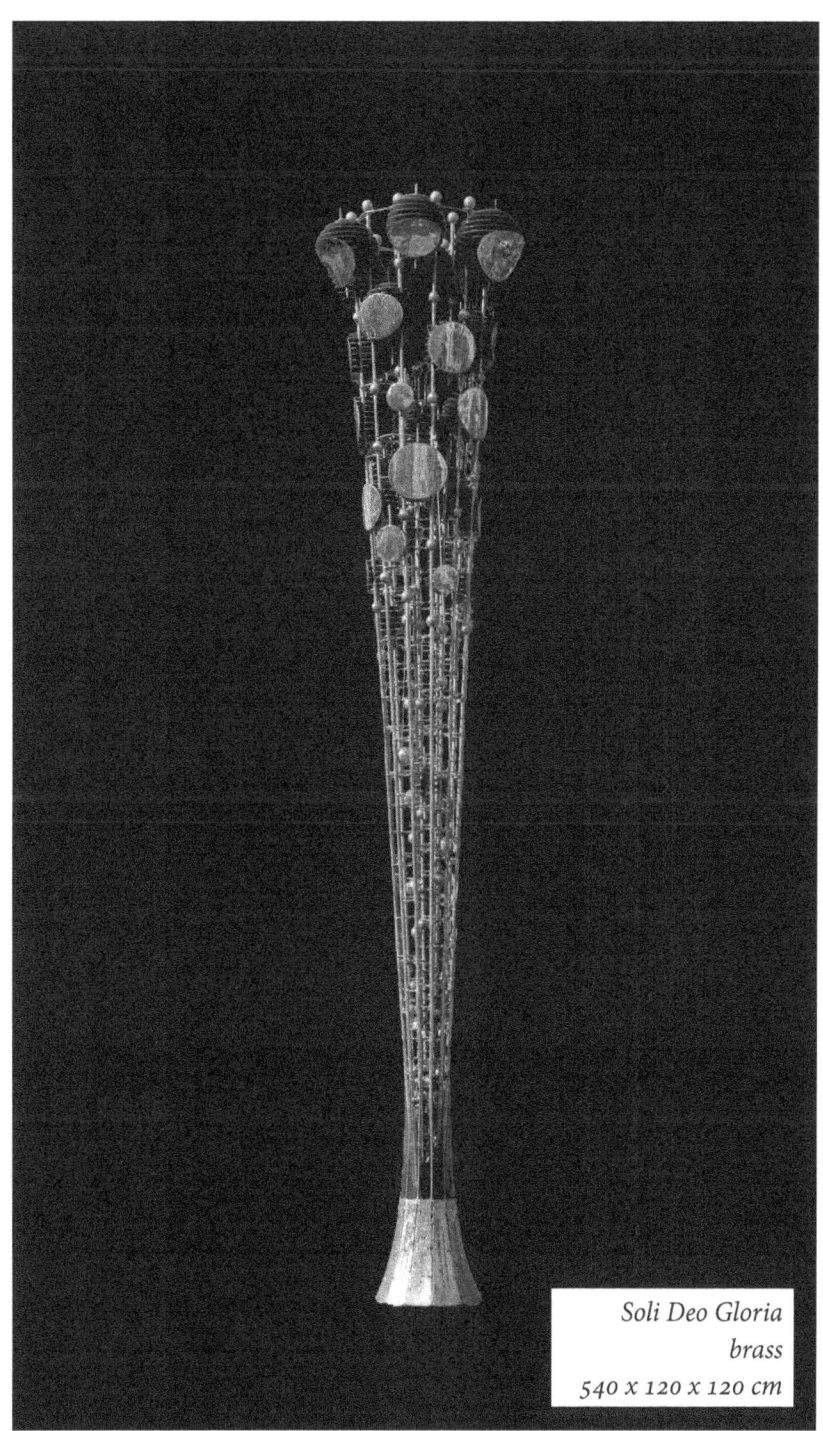

Soli Deo Gloria
brass
540 x 120 x 120 cm

The Trumpet in the Universe

The trumpet, however, stands
eighteen feet high outside the performance

hall, a glory of brass whirls
and small spheres on climbing rods,

like atoms merging, molecules of
planets. The trumpet is a mouthpiece

for which voice?
This trumpet,

its first making steadied by scaffolding
but now standing free. Silent

but at any moment music
could erupt connecting worlds.

> *You have fed us with the bread*
> *of tears, you have given us*
> *bowls of tears to drink.*

After so much repetition, the news feed's
monotone scandal is hardly scandalous.

We drift into complacencies,
safe from dire diagnoses (a cancer's 10% cure rate

after 5 years), intentional murders,
and random, politicians' lies, lost

aircraft, the gutter a blank margin
between facing pages. Or so we think.

Is there really an escape? Is God's voice
in the trumpet or the small silence?

And will joy—always a surprise—
splash fire flaring blaze

into corners dark with sorrows?

A Tombstone, the sixth archetype

The gravestone juts into the circle of the five solas,
the five archetypes, interrupting, as it always does,
breath, warm skin, eye beams, love, hate, the most
careful theology, even music. It is more than just
a granite slab but rather a stepping stone into the mansion
of what we have not seen, only imagined as vastly love-
filled space, a kingdom breaking into our troubled world.

We will step firmly, no vertigo in our resurrection flesh,
no tears, our bones reset and strong, our eyes open
not only to image but also to insight.

We are animated, all from nothing, nuclei, chromosomes,
genes, DNA, infused with movement, tempo, the beating
of the heart, the pinking of the skin, the soft breathing
of the sleeper breaking into wakefulness, eyes opening
to effortless light.

EPILOGUE

Oak
167 x 89 x 37 cm

**Altar for the book of words,
Altar for the book of nature**

These altars rise as monuments,
taller than can be reached
with no rungs for climbing.
The books are almost out of sight.
Teeming creation and the breathing word.

The word is story; its
pronouncement, "*Good.*"
It is two expelled, a father
with a knife for sacrifice,
the promise, the praise,

the darkness of the Psalms.
It is more than alphabet—thorns
dug into a forehead, the suffering,
the surprise of life again. The Word
is worded flesh, it is waters of flood,

of river, of baptism, of tears.
It is the one who says yes,
who gazes from the pages
written, to be read, to be
digested as if were eating them.
And creation speaks, too—
the parasitic strangleweed that knows
the plants around it by their smell.
Also the scarlet macaw, the red fox,
the yellow Indian bullfrog with bright

blue cheeks, the luna moth with the five-
inch wing span. The dahlias like small planets,
the bleeding heart, and all of the moss
trailing from ancient oaks.

> *You stretch out the heavens like a tent,*
> *you set the beams of your chambers on the waters,*
> *you make the clouds your chariot*
> *you ride on the wings of the wind,*
> *you make the winds your messengers,*
> *fire and flame your ministers.*

Poiesis
    —creator
        —the sculptor
            of the sculptor.

Notes

Prologue

l.26–29 Lines from the hymn, "Lord, It Belongs Not to My Care" by Richard Baxter (1615–1691).

Ascension I

l. 23 Stones of Brodgar: on the Orkney Islands, Scotland, the ring of Brodgar is a circle of massive stones similar to Stonehenge.

Ecce Homo!

l.30 P-38 https://en.wikipedia.org/wiki/Lockheed_P-38_Lightning. My father flew reconnaissance in a P-38 over Germany during World War II. His aircraft did not carry bombs—only cameras with which he took pictures before and after bombings. After his death we learned at Arlington that he flew 50 missions and volunteered for 50 more.

Golgotha

l. 47 "one poet of the 20th century": Wallace Stevens in his poem "Sunday Morning"

Heaven's Eyes

l. 2 Doctor R. J. Eckleburg: eyes on a billboard that brood over the wasteland in *The Great Gatsby* by F. Scot Fitzgerald

Tree of Love/Tree of Life

l. 13 ff   based on a sermon by Pastor David Lyle

Illseed

l. 18   from a sermon by Pastor Jeff Leininger

Shot Pillars

> Seven bronze pillars, each with a huge hole, stand in a plaza in Cluj-Napoca in Romania, Liviu Mocan's hometown, where 26 young men and women were shot by soldiers during the Romanian anticommunist Revolution.

Altar for the book of words, Altar for the book of nature

l. 29–34   from Ps 104: 2–4 RSV

Acknowledgments

THIS BOOK IS DEDICATED to Michael Wilder, Dean of the Conservatory of Music and Division of Arts and Communication at Wheaton College, who introduced me to the work of Liviu Mocan. His encouragement and enthusiasm for art and artists of the Word have supported our work and the work of so many other musicians and artists. We are immensely grateful. When I met Liviu some months later at the dedication of two of his sculptures placed in the lobby of the Armerding Arts Centre, our rapport was instantaneous. At lunch with our spouses that day we began to dream of a work of poetry inspired by his sculptures. I am immensely honored by his willingness to work with me—and by his suggestions all along the way. Without his stunning sculptures, these poems would have never happened—so in so many ways he through his work has been the Muse.

No words are sufficient for the encouragement and painstaking editing D.S. Martin (Don) gives and has given to each author in the Poiema Series—over 50 collections of poetry. I have had the good fortune now to have had two of my books included—and Don has been the editor every poet dreams of and so rarely has. A poet himself, he considers every word, every punctuation mark, the flow and meaning of each line. Without his clear vision and fine ear my poetry would have never become what it is.

Phillip Yancey's introduction and D.S. Martin's afterword previously appeared in *The McMaster Journal of Theology & Ministry*.

The photographs were provided by Radu Pop, Jonathan Tame, Liviu Mocan, John Ferguson, Dani Truta, Alex Rotea, and Baudouin Joachim. Many thanks for their beautiful work that enhances the poems.

Many thanks to the editors of the following publications for permission to reprint the following poems in this collection:

"Golgotha" published as "Death is the Mother of Beauty" in Jill Peláez Baumgaertner, *From Shade to Shine: New Poems* (Paraclete Press)

"After the Annunciation: *The Second Adam*" published in *A Radiant Birth: Advent Readings for a Bright Season,* ed. Leslie Leyland Fields and Paul J. Willis, Intervarsity Press, 2023.

"The Birth of Stained Glass" to be published in future issue of *Christianity and Literature.*

"Sunday Morning I," "Sunday Morning II," and "Sunday Morning III," in *Presence: A Journal of Catholic Poetry,* 2023.

"Sunday Morning IV," published as "Easter, Before It's Noticed" in Jill Peláez Baumgaertner, *Shade and Shine: New Poems* (Paraclete Press)

The Five Solas were published online in Artway https://artway.eu/artway.php?id=1288&lang=en&action=show

"Seed Among thorns" appeared in the online journal, *Ekstasis.*

The Poiema Poetry Series

COLLECTIONS IN THIS SERIES INCLUDE:

Six Sundays Toward a Seventh by Sydney Lea
Epitaphs for the Journey by Paul Mariani
Within This Tree of Bones by Robert Siegel
Particular Scandals by Julie L. Moore
Gold by Barbara Crooker
A Word In My Mouth by Robert Cording
Say This Prayer into the Past by Paul Willis
Scape by Luci Shaw
Conspiracy of Light by D.S. Martin
Second Sky by Tania Runyan
Remembering Jesus by John Leax
What Cannot Be Fixed by Jill Pelaez Baumgaertner
Still Working It Out by Brad Davis
The Hatching of the Heart by Margo Swiss
Collage of Seoul by Jae Newman
Twisted Shapes of Light by William Jolliff
These Intricacies by David Harrity
Where the Sky Opens by Laurie Klein
True, False, None of the Above by Marjorie Maddox
The Turning Aside anthology edited by D.S. Martin
Falter by Marjorie Stelmach
Phases by Mischa Willett
Second Bloom by Anya Krugovoy Silver
Adam, Eve, & the Riders of the Apocalypse anthology edited by D.S. Martin
Your Twenty-First Century Prayer Life by Nathaniel Lee Hansen
Habitation of Wonder by Abigail Carroll

Ampersand by D.S. Martin
Full Worm Moon by Julie L. Moore
Ash & Embers by James A. Zoller
The Book of Kells by Barbara Crooker
Reaching Forever by Philip C. Kolin
The Book of Bearings by Diane Glancy
In a Strange Land anthology edited by D.S. Martin
What I Have I Offer With Two Hands by Jacob Stratman
Slender Warble by Susan Cowger
Madonna, Complex by Jen Stewart Fueston
No Reason by Jack Stewart
Abundance by Andrew Lansdown
Angelicus by D.S. Martin
Trespassing on the Mount of Olives by Brad Davis
The Angel of Absolute Zero by Marjorie Stelmach
Duress by Karen An-hwei Lee
Wolf Intervals by Graham Hillard
To Heaven's Rim anthology edited by Burl Horniachek
Cup My Days Like Water by Abigail Carroll
Soon Done with the Crosses by Claude Wilkinson
House of 49 Doors by Laurie Klein
Hawk and Songbird by Susan Cowger
Ponds by J. C. Scharl
The Farewell Suites by Andrew Lansdown
Let's Call It Home by Luke Harvey
Forbearance by Cameron Brooks

www.ingramcontent.com/pod-product-compliance
Lightning Source LLC
Chambersburg PA
CBHW051656040426
42446CB00009B/1171